Who? Me ....

Larry Judd
2021

Larry is the author of the following books:

You Can't Judge a Book By It's Cover

Preparation Time

Preachers' Planner 2017 – 2018

Preachers' Planner 2019 – 2020

Is The Catholic Church the True Church?

The Heart of a Shepherd

Complaint Cultures

Larry's formal education includes:

B.S.E.	Oklahoma Christian College
M.Ed.	Central State University
Innovative Leadership Program	The University of Alabama
Ed.S.	Lincoln Memorial University

Graduate of the Chattanooga School of Preaching & Biblical Studies

He is married to Cheryl Buchanan Judd. They have two grown sons, two wonderful daughters-in-laws, and four tremendous grandchildren.

Larry is a retired teacher with 35 years' experiences, 24 of those years he was also coaching.

He has 6 years' experiences as a youth director.
He has 13 years' experiences preaching.
He has served as a deacon at the East Ridge church of Christ.
He currently serves as an elder at the Ooltewah church of Christ.

Larry has done mission work on the Navajo Reservation, Russia, Philippines, and Belize.

First Printing: 2021

Larry Judd
4588 Cherokee Valley Rd.
Ringgold, GA 30736

larryjudd.preacher@gmail.com

Art Work: Inera Isovic

ISBN: 9798712807048

Contents

Preface

This year, 2021, in many ways seems to be a continuation of 2020! Covid, staying home much of the time, masks, and social distancing. However, there have been some changes ... vaccinations, the unrest in our nation, the election is history, and the news' networks are depressing.

Therefore, an escape, using time for a good purpose, is the study of the Bible, praying, and writing.

As you read, *Who? Me ...*, I hope it offers encouragement. I hope it can be used as a tool in studying your Bible. I hope you can come to the realization that God can use, even the most "insignificant" among us. Yet, really ... none are "insignificant", because we are created in the image of God.

We know of characters from the Bible such as Abraham, Noah, Moses, Paul, Peter, James, and John. However, as you read *Who? Me ...*, I hope you will be introduced or reminded of some people we find in the word of God, that are not the "prominent" people, yet very valuable, very useful, very respected, and some very great lessons from them.

The power is in the word of God. Romans 1: 16, " For I am not ashamed of the gospel [a]of Christ, for it is the power of God to salvation for everyone who believes, for the Jew first and also for the Greek." (NKJV)

It would be very presumptuous on my part, and wrong, to think that this book would be equivalent or supersede the Bible. I hope that this book can be used as a tool in your studying the Bible.

All quotations from the Scriptures will be from the New King James

Version, unless otherwise stated.

I want to thank Inera Isovic for the photography used for the cover of this book. I really like the photo of the lighthouse. I think it is appropriate for **Who? Me …**, because it can help us remember that as Christians, each of us needs to let our lights shine. It doesn't matter our prestige in life, how much our bank account says we have. It doesn't matter what our portfolio of investments looks like. Those who have been obedient to Jesus, His commands, added to His one church, are one in Christ Jesus. Jesus said in Matthew 5: 13 – 16, "You are the salt of the earth; but if the salt loses its flavor, how shall it be seasoned? It is then good for nothing but to be thrown out and trampled underfoot by men.

[14] "You are the light of the world. A city that is set on a hill cannot be hidden. [15] Nor do they light a lamp and put it under a basket, but on a lampstand, and it gives light to all *who are* in the house. [16] Let your light so shine before men, that they may see your good works and glorify your Father in heaven."

As you study the Bible, looking at the characters found in the Scriptures, may it give you courage, strength, and encouragement.

I pray that this book will be a blessing to you in your study of the word of God, the Bible.

In HIM,
Larry Judd

Chapter 1: Introduction

Chapter 1 is called "Introduction" for a few reasons:

1. It isn't about one of the characters in the Bible.

2. It allows me to introduce you to some of my heritage.

3. I want it to be a reminder to my sons.

4. I want it to be information that my grandchildren will cherish.

I am Larry Judd, the son of Dee and Wanda Judd. My maternal grandparents were Columbus and Anis Satterfield. So, my grandpa was William Columbus Satterfield.

Grandpa was born February 10, 1906, and passed away May 18, 1991. Grandpa and Grandma were faithful members of the church of Christ.

Grandpa had a 6th grade education, as he had to quit school to support the family. Grandpa only had a 6th grade education, but he was a very wise man!

Grandpa always said he was the fourth smartest in his class, because there were only four in the class.

Was my grandpa perfect? No. The only perfect man who walked on the face of the earth, was Jesus Christ. No, my grandpa was not perfect, but he was a great man.

Grandpa grew up during the "Great Depression" years; difficult years, but a time when neighbors looked out for one another, helped one another, and cared for one another.

Grandpa was a farmer and an oil well pumper. (An Oklahoma oil well pumper, had oil wells that he had to hand crank to get them started. When the wells did not have a cut-off, he would have to go back and shut them down in the late afternoon. He would have to climb a stairwell up the oil tanks, and let a gauge, like a plum-line, drop down to measure the oil production.) Grandpa was meticulous. He kept the grounds around the wells he was pumping clear of weeds and stickers.

Grandpa taught me how to drive. Driving on those old country, gravel roads, with bar ditches on either side. As I was preparing to take my driver's test, I was out with Grandpa and I was driving his pickup truck to the oil wells. One particular one was about a quarter of a mile, down a rutted drive. We got to that well, and Grandpa got it started. He got in the truck and told me to back it up … back it up that quarter of a mile. I did so. Then, Grandpa told me to drive it forward to the well. I did. Then, back it up. Pull forward. Then, my Grandpa with his quiet wisdom said, "Larry, if you can drive backwards, you can drive forwards. Anyone can drive forwards." (Valuable lesson.)

Grandpa had a black smith shop in his garage area; forge, anvil, hammers, and tongs. The neighbors brought their broken equipment to Grandpa to fix. They would bring their flat tires to Grandpa to fix. I NEVER heard my grandpa quote a price for his work for any of these repairs! When they would ask what they owed him, my grandpa would say, "Oh, whatever it's worth to you."

After my Grandpa and Grandma retired from the farm to the city of Tulsa, near my mom and dad, Grandpa had a pile of scrap iron

2

stacked by their deck. One day I asked Grandpa, "Grandpa, why do you have all that iron stacked up out there?" Grandpa's response, "Larry, you never know when someone may need something." (Valuable lesson)

Grandpa taught me about working on the farm, feeding the cows, driving a tractor, raking hay, helping carry irrigation pipe from one place to another in a meadow after the hay had been cut and baled.

The only time I can remember my Grandpa getting irritated at me was when I got the rake caught in a gate, while pulling it with the tractor to move the equipment from the hayfield back to the farm.

He didn't even get angry or upset the time I was driving in a hayfield, with Grandpa standing on the running board of the truck, and I hit a hole, and knocked him off the truck.

Let me jump ahead a little, in the later years of Grandpa's life he was diabetic and had to have a leg amputated. That didn't stop Grandpa. He and Grandma continued to go fishing. He continued making his way down the driveway to get to the basement, where his workshop was. He continued to use his welding machine. Sparks would be flying, and I was concerned that Grandpa was going to burn up his artificial leg.

When you came into the house where they retired, you came into the living room. To the right, was the dining room, through it was the kitchen. Adjacent to the kitchen was a bedroom, and next to it was another bedroom, and that opened up to the living room. So, it made sort of a circle. After I was married and my wife and I had our children, my sister had her children, and we were at Grandma and Grandpa's. The kids got to playing and running around that circle. (It was driving me nuts.) Grandpa was sitting in his wheel chair in the living room, just taking it all in. I asked him, "Grandpa, doesn't that bother you?". His response, "I just enjoy watching them play."

(Patience – a valuable lesson.)

Grandpa grew up in a generation, where the words "I love you." were rare. However, there was never a doubt of my Grandpa's love.

Back to the farm years. Grandpa and Grandma always put in a big garden. Gardening was a family ordeal. When it was time to pick the corn, we were all involved. When it came time to pick the beans, we were all involved. When it came time to dig up the peanuts, we were all involved. When potatoes were dug up, we were all involved.

These were days when you didn't go to the store to buy chicken out of the "meat section" of the grocery store. No, killing chickens and preparing them for the freezer, or for a meal that day, was a family ordeal. Grandpa would prepare a big 50-gallon drum of water, with a fire under it. Grandpa would catch the chickens, bring them to Grandma, where she would put a crow bar on their necks and wring the necks. The chickens would flop around, bleeding out, when they would be caught, mom and dad would dunk them in that hot water. Then our job was to start plucking the feathers. (If you have never smelled wet chicken feathers ... it is bad!) After they were plucked, they were taken inside where Grandma and Mom would cut them into pieces.

Family time … working together … sharing responsibilities. (Valuable lessons.)

We lived in Tulsa, Oklahoma, and Grandma and Grandpa lived on the farm in Yale, Oklahoma – about 50 miles away. We would go to Grandma and Grandpa's about twice a month. In the summers, my sister and I would stay for 2 weeks with Grandma and Grandpa. It didn't matter what time we arrived at Grandma and Grandpa's, the first question my Grandpa would always ask, "Have you eaten, yet?"

I recently found out a story about my grandpa. It was winter, and his sister-in-law was going into labor. There was snow on the ground and covering the roads. Grandpa got the tractor out, and drove on the roads, making ruts, to make sure the doctor could get to the house. (For those younger ones, reading the book, yes in those days, going to the hospital was a rarity, even to have a baby.) The relative that was born was the one who shared this story.

During the Depression, being a farmer, Grandpa got a larger gas ration. When my mom was a girl in school, her teacher's fiancée was in the military, and stationed at a base, miles away. Grandpa would give gas rations to my mom's teacher, so that she could make the trip on a weekend to visit her fiancée.

Whenever a relative was sick, Grandpa and Grandma would house them, care for them, and help them regain health.

Following church services, Grandpa and Grandma would invite the preacher out to their house to eat. (Maybe the preacher and his family would just show up, and that was just fine.)

(Generosity, benevolence, sharing, caring – valuable lessons.)

5

I never heard Grandpa lead a public prayer. At a younger age, Grandpa had pneumonia, so I never heard Grandpa sing. I never heard Grandpa preach a sermon. I never heard Grandpa do a public Bible reading. I never saw Grandpa serve communion for the Lord's Supper.

However, this was before the days of "Weed-Eaters". Grass was trimmed by getting down on your knees and pulling the grass. That's what Grandpa did around the church building. Grandpa made sure the flower beds at the church building were weeded. Grandpa was the one out painting stripes on a hot asphalt parking lot at the church building. Grandpa and my dad were up in the hot attic of the church building, having to pull air conditioning pipes.

When it came to housing for youth rallies or other youth events, Grandma and Grandpa's house was always available.

When it came time to host youth devotionals, Grandma and Grandpa's house was always available.

(Service; private, behind the scenes, not necessarily a "five-talent man", but using the abilities that God had given – valuable lessons.)

Towards the end of Grandpa's life, it was very interesting to watch him intently reading his Bible. I thought, you know, he's finding out about his new neighbors.

The stories and the fond memories could go on and on!

However, this is an introduction to my background, my heritage. A reason that this chapter fits in, is because Grandpa was not one for being out front. He was not a public figure. He was quiet, yet a faithful servant. Even though he didn't have much of a public education, he had such great wisdom, and left such valuable lessons. Grandpa's legacy is wonderful! My sister and I, his grandchildren, will never forget Grandpa. His great grandchildren were young when he died, however maybe they will remember some about Grandpa Satterfield, and if they can't remember, maybe reading this chapter will share some great stories about him. His great-great grandchildren never had the opportunity to meet Grandpa Satterfield. However, some of them live in the area where he lived, in fact on property that he owned. Even though they didn't know Grandpa Satterfield, I hope that they can see some valuable lessons that live on with his legacy in his grandchildren, my sister and I.

Questions

1. Who was an influential person in your life?

2. What valuable lesson(s) did you learn from that person?

3. How powerful is influence?

4. How can we improve "family time"?

5. What legacy do you want to leave?

Chapter 2: A Young Captive Girl

Imagine a young girl, taken captive, taken to a foreign land, and in servitude. What would be the attitude?

- Bitterness

- Homesickness

- Sullenness

- Quietness

- Isolation

Those characteristics and actions could be completely understood. However, not in the case of this particular young girl.

What was her name?

- We don't know.

How old was she?

- We don't know.

This young girl seems to be pretty obscure. However, what a powerful influence she had for God. What a powerful influence she had upon the woman she served. What an influence she had upon the woman's husband. What an indirect influence upon the king.

The young girl that I am describing is found in 2nd Kings 5.

2nd Kings 5: 1 – 14, "Now Naaman, commander of the army of the king of Syria, was a great and honorable man in the eyes of his master, because by him the Lord had given victory to Syria. He was also a mighty man of valor, *but* a leper. **2** And the Syrians had gone out on[a] raids, and had brought back captive a young girl from the land of Israel. She [b]waited on Naaman's wife. **3** Then she said to her mistress, "If only my master *were* with the prophet who *is* in Samaria! For he would heal him of his leprosy." **4** And *Naaman* went in and told his master, saying, "Thus and thus said the girl who *is* from the land of Israel."

5 Then the king of Syria said, "Go now, and I will send a letter to the king of Israel."

So he departed and took with him ten talents of silver, six thousand *shekels* of gold, and ten changes of clothing. **6** Then he brought the letter to the king of Israel, which said,

Now be advised, when this letter comes to you, that I have sent Naaman my servant to you, that you may heal him of his leprosy.

7 And it happened, when the king of Israel read the letter, that he tore his clothes and said, "*Am* I God, to kill and make alive, that this man sends a man to me to heal him of his leprosy? Therefore please consider, and see how he seeks a quarrel with me."

8 So it was, when Elisha the man of God heard that the king of Israel had torn his clothes, that he sent to the king, saying, "Why have you torn your clothes? Please let him come to me, and he shall know that there is a prophet in Israel."

9 Then Naaman went with his horses and chariot, and he stood at the door of Elisha's house. **10** And Elisha sent a messenger to him, saying, "Go and wash in the Jordan seven times, and your flesh shall be restored to you, and *you shall* be clean." **11** But Naaman became furious, and went away and said, "Indeed, I said to myself, 'He will surely come out *to me,* and stand and call on the name of the Lord his God, and wave his hand over the place, and heal the leprosy.' **12** *Are* not the [c]Abanah and the Pharpar, the rivers of Damascus, better than all the waters of Israel? Could I not wash in them and be clean?" So he turned and went away in a rage. **13** And his servants came near and spoke to him, and said, "My father, *if* the prophet had told you *to do* something great, would you not have done *it?* How much more then, when he says to you, 'Wash, and be clean'?" **14** So he went down and dipped seven times in the Jordan, according to the saying of the man of God; and his flesh was restored like the flesh of a little child, and he was clean."

What if this young girl would have thought, "Who? Me…" What can I do to help this situation? These people have taken me captive. They have made me to be a servant. Why should I help? What can I do?

Thankfully, this was NOT her attitude!

"The unsung heroine of this whole narrative is this precious little girl who had been captured by the Syrians and made a slave to the house of Naaman. Instead of becoming bitter against her exploiters and harboring an undying hatred of them, she accepted her fate with meekness and exhibited deep friendship and sympathy with her mistress and her husband, Naaman.

It was this captive maiden who enlightened the great lord of the Syrian armies of the existence of a true prophet of God in Samaria and of his ability to cure leprosy.

What an exhortation is this for everyone to seize all opportunities to speak of God and His great power to benefit sinful and suffering humanity! Through the word of this servant girl, the king of Syria received the knowledge of a true prophet of God in Samaria, information which was not even known (because of his own fault) by the king of Israel (Joram). (Coffman)

Notice the positive characteristics of Naaman:

- Commander of the army of the king of Syria

- Great man

- Honorable man

- Because of him, the Lord had given victory to Syria

- Mighty man of valor

Then comes the severe negative:

- "… but a leper."

"Many have thought leprosy to be a disease of the skin. It is better classified, however, as a disease of the nervous system because the leprosy bacterium attacks the nerves. Leprosy's agent *M. leprae* is a rod-shaped bacterium related to the tuberculosis bacterium. Leprosy is spread by multiple skin contacts, as well as by droplets from the upper respiratory tracts, such as nasal secretions that are transmitted from person to person.

Its symptoms start in the skin and peripheral nervous system (outside the brain and spinal cord), then spread to other parts, such as the hands, feet, face, and earlobes. Patients with leprosyexperience disfigurement of the skin and bones, twisting of the limbs, and curling of the fingers to form the characteristic claw hand. Facial changes include thickening of the outer ear and collapsing of the nose.

Tumor-like growths called lepromas may form on the skin and in the respiratory tract, and the optic nerve may deteriorate. The largest number of deformities develop from loss of pain sensation due to extensive nerve damage. For instance, inattentive patients can pick up a cup of boiling water without flinching." (Gillen)

This young girl, a captive of the Syrians, who waited on Naaman's wife, did not remain quiet. She had the courage, the conviction, and the rapport to speak to Naaman's wife, "If only my master were with the prophet who is in Samaria! For he would heal him of his leprosy." (verse 3)

See the ripple effect of this young girls' influence:

- To Naaman's wife

- To Naaman

- To the king

Naaman was sent to the prophet, and allowed his own thoughts almost get in the way of his healing. The prophet sent a messenger to him, telling Naaman to go and wash in the Jordan River, seven times.

Naaman thought the prophet would surely come out!

Naaman thought the prophet would stand, call on the name of the Lord, wave his hand over the place, and heal him of the dreaded disease.

That did NOT happen, and Naaman was furious. He left, having in his own mind how the healing should have taken place; and besides weren't the rivers in Damascus much better than that Jordan River?

Fortunately, Naaman had servants who cared enough for him to bring it to his attention, that if the prophet would have told him some great thing to do, wouldn't he had done it. So, Naaman went to the Jordan River, and in complete obedience, dipped the seven times. When he came up from dipping the seventh time, "... his flesh was restored like the flesh of a little child, and he was clean." (verse 14)

What if it had not been for this young girl ...

- The one who was taken captive

- The one who was in a foreign country

- The one who was serving Naaman's wife

- The one who was willing to speak up for the prophet, Elisha

- The one who had the rapport to be trusted

- The one who's influence was not only to Naaman's wife, but to Naaman, and to the king.

- The persuasion from Naaman's servants for him to obey what he had been told to do from Elisha's messenger.

So, we have the great lessons of the power of God, complete obedience, not according to our own thoughts, but what we are commanded from the word of God.

Stop and think ... none of this would have happened, (from this account) had it not been for a young, captive girl. One who did NOT have an attitude of "Who? Me ...", but rather took a stand, showed courage, conviction, and told where the answer for the healing of Naaman could be found.

Great things were accomplished from the actions of a young girl who many might have considered very insignificant ... this was a captive, a servant, a young girl.

Yet, God used this young person to spread some wonderful news, and God performed mighty actions in the healing of Naaman.

Questions

1. What "ripple effects" have you seen in sharing the gospel of Christ?

2. How can we encourage our young people to use opportunities to stand for God?

3. What are some excuses people make in delaying obedience to God?

4. What are some things people do to put their own opinions and ideas ahead of what God commands?

5. Discuss the relief and joy of being cleansed.

Chapter 3: The Mariners

Mariners, sailors, rugged men, strong men, burley men, men who believed and prayed to gods.

- What were their names?

  o Don't know.

- How many were there?

  o Don't know.

- How old were they?

  o Don't know.

Not knowing their names, how many there were, nor their names … not knowing a lot, yet from these "obscure" men, we can learn much.

The men, the mariners, the sailors are those found in Jonah chapter 1. The word of the Lord came to Jonah, a prophet of God, to go to Nineveh, a great city, and cry out against it. Nineveh was not only a large city, it was a wicked city. "But Jonah", verse 3, decided to reject the word of the Lord, thereby reject the Lord, reject his responsibility to proclaim the word of the Lord, and reject Nineveh. He decided to go as far away, in the opposite direction, as he could in getting away from his assignment to Nineveh. He paid the fare, got on a boat going to Tarshish, and tried to run away from the Lord.

Obviously boats during that time did not have big, strong, mechanical engines to power the boat. They were propelled by manual labor. Therefore, these men had to have strong muscles. These sailors, mariners, men of the sea would have strength and stamina, and experiences from sea episodes.

This "stranger" has gotten on board, and gone down into the ship, and gone to sleep. However, in the meantime, the mariners were battling a fierce storm. A storm so strong that these experienced men of the sea became fearful, because the ship was about to be broken up. (They did not realize at the time that the storm was from God.)

"Then the mariners were afraid; and every man cried out to his god, and threw the cargo that was in the ship into the sea, to lighten the load. But Jonah had gone down into the lowest parts of the ship, had lain down, and was fast asleep." (verse 5)

- The mariners were afraid

- The mariners cried out to his god

- The mariners threw the cargo into the sea

Notice, they cried out to "his god", little "g", a false god. How long had they believed in this "god"? We don't know; however, "every man cried out to his god,".

The captain of the ship, went down to Jonah and said, "What do you mean, sleeper? Arise, call on your God; perhaps your God will consider us, so that we may not perish." (verse 6)

This captain realized that there was a difference between Jonah's God and their god.

"And they said to one another, 'Come, let us cast lots, that we may know for whose cause this trouble has come upon us.' So they cast lots, and the lot fell on Jonah." (verse 7)

Then the barrage of questions came as they exhorted Jonah, "Please tell us!" (verse 8)

- "For whose cause is this trouble upon us?"

19

- "What is your occupation?"

- "And where do you come from"

- "What is your country?"

- "And of what people are you?"

Valid questions, as they are fearing the storm and the breaking up of the ship.

Jonah answered their questions, verse 9.

- "I am a Hebrew"

- "I fear the Lord, the God of heaven, who made the sea and dry land."

A brief explanation, and a very short "sermon" about the existence of God, but watch the results!

"Then the men were exceedingly afraid, and said to him, "Why have you done this?" For the men knew that he fled from the presence of the Lord, because he had told them. [11] Then they said to him, "What shall we do to you that the sea may be calm for us?"—for the sea was growing more tempestuous.

[12] And he said to them, "Pick me up and [d]throw me into the sea; then the sea will become calm for you. For I know that this great tempest *is* because of me." (Verses 10 – 12)

Imagine the thoughts that could have run through their heads … throw this man overboard? What, let us suffer for being guilty of his blood being on our hands?

So, watch what they did … "Nevertheless the men rowed hard to return to land, but they could not, for the sea continued to grow more tempestuous against them." (Verse 13)

Remember, it was mentioned of the changes in these mariners.

- They had believed in a god.

- Each cried out to "his god".

Watch …

"Therefore they cried out to the Lord and said, "We pray, O Lord, please do not let us perish for this man's life, and do not charge us with innocent blood; for You, O Lord, have done as it pleased You." **15** So they picked up Jonah and threw him into the sea, and the sea ceased from its raging. **16** Then the men feared the Lord exceedingly, and offered a sacrifice to the Lord and took vows." (verses 14 – 16)

- "They cried out to the Lord"

- "We pray, O Lord"

- ".. for You, O Lord, have done as it pleased You."

- "Then the men feared the Lord exceedingly"

- ".. and offered a sacrifice to the Lord and took vows"

These men did a 180 degree turn.

Then, we have the rest of the story of Jonah, eventually going to Nineveh, the repentance of Nineveh, and Jonah needing to continue to learn some valuable lessons.

However, notice the valuable lessons we can learn from the men, who we don't even know their names, their ages, or even how many of them were on that ship.

- No matter the circumstances

- No matter your environment

- No matter how you were raised

- No matter what you believed before

It's not too late to make a 180 degree turn, and follow after the true and living God!

You may be facing some terrible, strong storms in the ship called life. The storms seem so strong, they are about to tear you up.

It's not too late!

The environment you are in may be rough, shady, crimes rampant, cries of pain from abuse, smell of alcohol, weed, needles laying on the sidewalk.

It's not too late!

You may have been raised in a family that didn't even believe in God. You may never have even heard of God. Or, you may have been one of those "C.E.M." people … only going to some church on Christmas, Easter, and Mother's Day. (That's far from demonstrating true obedience and faithfulness to the Lord.)

It's not too late!

Your family may have had conviction, sincerity, zeal, … however, following after "your god"; whether the god of …

22

- Convenience

- Family heritage

- Popularity

- Immorality

- Self-indulgence

- Self-gratification

- Work

- Sports

- Finances

- Cars

- Houses

- Etc., Etc., Etc.

It's not too late!

As long as we are breathing, cognizant, able to make decisions …

It's not too late!

These unknown mariners made a 180 degree turn and so can we.

The Lord does not want any to perish!

2nd Peter 3: 9, "The Lord is not slack concerning *His* promise, as some count slackness, but is longsuffering toward [a]us, not willing that any should perish but that all should come to repentance."

It is NOT what we think, NOT our way, NOT how we want to follow HIM, but what does He say?. We must make that 180 degree turn and follow Him, as He commands.

Reader, please allow me to ask a question. Do you love Jesus? (Only you can answer that question.)

If the answer is "yes", then notice what Jesus said in John 14: 15, "If you love Me, keep My commandments.".

So, what are the commands of Jesus? (Please don't take my word for it, look at the passages yourself, and see if it is what Jesus said.)

Jesus said that we must:

- Hear (Matthew 7: 24 – 27)

- Believe (John 8: 24)

- Repent (Luke 13: 3, 5)

- Confess (Matthew 10: 32, 33)

- Be Baptized (Mark 16: 15 – 16)

- Remain Faithful (Revelation 2: 10b)

It's not too late!

When a person is baptized into Christ for the forgiveness of their sins, the Lord adds that person to His one church. (Acts 2: 47)

(If you would like to discuss this further, you have my e-mail address in the front of the book, or contact a church of Christ in your local area.)

It's not too late!

Questions

1. How can fear be a motivator?

2. How do people try to run away from God today?

3. What are some 180 degree changes you have seen in people?

4. What approach do you use to those who are brought up in denominationalism?

5. How do you encourage people that it is not too late to obey God?

Chapter 4: A Lad

Young people may think, "Who? Me ..." "What can I do?" "I am just a young person."

Paul wrote to the young man Timothy in 1st Timothy 4: 12, "Let no one [a]despise your youth, but be an example to the believers in word, in conduct, in love, [b]in spirit, in faith, in purity."

Think about what King Saul told the young shepherd boy, David, as David said he would go out and face the giant, Goliath. "And Saul said to David, 'You are not able to go against this Philistine to fight with him; for you are a youth, and he a man of war from his youth." (1st Samuel 17: 33)

To paraphrase; Saul said "you can't", but he has "from his youth".

Wait! I can't, but he has. What type of mixed message does that give?

In this chapter, we want to study an obscure, unknown by name, lad.

John 6: 1 – 14, "After these things Jesus went over the Sea of Galilee, which is *the Sea* of Tiberias. ² Then a great multitude followed Him, because they saw His signs which He performed on those who were diseased.[a] ³ And Jesus went up on the mountain, and there He sat with His disciples.

⁴ Now the Passover, a feast of the Jews, was near. ⁵ Then Jesus lifted up *His* eyes, and seeing a great multitude coming toward Him, He said to Philip, "Where shall we buy bread, that these may eat?" ⁶ But this He said to test him, for He Himself knew what He would do.

⁷ Philip answered Him, "Two hundred denarii worth of bread is not

sufficient for them, that every one of them may have a little."

8 One of His disciples, Andrew, Simon Peter's brother, said to Him, **9** "There is a lad here who has five barley loaves and two small fish, but what are they among so many?"

10 Then Jesus said, "Make the people sit down." Now there was much grass in the place. So the men sat down, in number about five thousand. **11** And Jesus took the loaves, and when He had given thanks He distributed *them* [b]to the disciples, and the disciples to those sitting down; and likewise of the fish, as much as they wanted. **12** So when they were filled, He said to His disciples, "Gather up the fragments that remain, so that nothing is lost." **13** Therefore they gathered *them* up, and filled twelve baskets with the fragments of the five barley loaves which were left over by those who had eaten. **14** Then those men, when they had seen the sign that Jesus did, said, "This is truly the Prophet who is to come into the world."

Often, when this passage is studied, emphasis is given; not only to Jesus and His power, but also to Andrew; the one who was bringing people to Jesus. He brought his brother, Simon, to Jesus (John 1: 40 – 42). In this passage, Andrew is bringing a lad to Jesus with five barley loaves and two small fish.

However, I would like for us to focus on the lad. This boy was among the multitude of people. The multitude numbered about five thousand men (Mark 6: 44), and that's not counting the women and children.

- What was his name?

    o We don't know that.

- Who were his parents?

    o We don't know that.

28

- How old was he?

    o We don't know that.

- How did Andrew find him, with so many people?

    o We don't know that.

Many "we don't know that" answers. However, there are some very valuable lessons that can be learned.

1. The boy was willing to give what he had for Jesus to use. No matter how meagre it seemed in comparison to such a large multitude; five barley loaves and two small fish. Even Andrew questioned, "... but what are they among so many?" (John 6: 9)

2. Jesus can take the insignificant and perform the significant. When the boy gave what he had, "And Jesus took the loaves, and when He had given thanks He distributed them to the disciples, and the disciples to those sitting down; and likewise of the fish, as much as they wanted." (verse 11)

3. The boy had a part in many realizing who Jesus was. The people ate and were filled. There were twelve baskets filled with the left overs. "Then those men, when they had seen the sign that Jesus did, said, 'This is truly the Prophet who is to come into the world.'" (verse 14) Think ... if the boy had not given his five loaves and two small fish, this miracle would not have been done. These men would not have seen this miracle. Yet, the boy gave, Jesus gave thanks and performed a miracle, they ate and were filled, and the men came to the conclusion "This is truly the Prophet who is to come into the world."

- A person may feel insignificant. Jesus can use that person.

- What that person gives may seem insignificant. Jesus can use what they give.

In this particular case, we are learning from a lad. However, it doesn't matter the age, nor the amount as long as it is according "as he may proper," (1st Corinthians 16: 2), and that the glory goes to God.

We have an almighty, powerful, omniscient, omnipresent, omnipotent God. We need to love Him, obey Him, follow Him, and serve Him.

Paul wrote in Philippians 4: 19, "And my God shall supply all your need according to His riches in glory by Christ Jesus."

Paul also wrote in Ephesians 3: 20, "Now to Him who is able to do exceedingly abundantly above all that we ask or think, according to the power that works in us,"

Our God is powerful!

- If Paul would have written, God is able to do more than we are; we would have known that God is greater than we are. However, that's not what Paul wrote.

- If Paul would have written, God is able to do exceedingly more than us; we would have known that God is greater than we are. However, that's not all Paul wrote.

- If Paul would have written, God is able to do exceedingly abundantly more than us; we would have known God is greater than we are. However, that's not all Paul wrote.

Notice what Paul did write, "Now to Him who is able to do exceedingly abundantly above all that we ask or think, according to the power that works in us,"

- Exceedingly

- Abundantly

- Above

- All that we ask or think

Our God is powerful!

The age of miracles has ended. The purpose of the miracles was to confirm the word of God. (Mark 16: 20). The miracles were passed on by the laying on of the apostles' hands. (Acts 8: 14 – 18). The people who the apostles laid their hands on could not pass the miracles on to others. So, there was a phasing out of the miraculous gifts. There are no physically living apostles today, nor people who they laid their hands upon; therefore, no miracles being performed. Also, we read in 1st Corinthians 13: 10, "But when that which is perfect has come, then that which is in part will be done away." "... when that which is perfect has come ..." What does the "perfect" in this passage mean? Some would quickly answer, Jesus. Jesus was perfect, sinless, blameless. However, Jesus is masculine gender. Does the passage say, When He who is perfect is come? No. Masculine gender is not used in the verse, but rather neuter gender; that which is neither masculine nor feminine. "Perfect" in this passage is meaning, "complete". So, the neuter gender, complete is referring to the word of God, the Scriptures. 2nd Timothy 3: 16 – 17, "All Scripture *is* given by inspiration of God, and *is* profitable for doctrine, for reproof, for correction, for [a]instruction in righteousness, [17] that the man of God may be complete, thoroughly equipped for every good work."

31

We have the inspired, word of God. We can read of the miracles that took place. God's power is not diminished. In fact, we read in Romans 1: 16, "For I am not ashamed of the gospel of Christ, for it is the power of God to salvation for everyone who believes, for the Jew first and also for the Greek."

There is a difference between wondrous things, and miracles. Miracles were in the realm of the supernatural. However, wondrous things, can be great things that are existent, even today … answers to prayers, God's providence in action, accomplishments for the glory of God.

Two of our four grandchildren were born prematurely. One was thirteen weeks early, another fifteen weeks early. There were many prayers offered and answered. The NICU staffs were remarkable. Today, at the time of writing this book, one is thirteen years old, the other eight years old. This is powerful, wondrous, however, in the true since of the word … not miraculous.

Back to the lad in John 6 … we can learn that:

- God can use people of different ages.

- God can use what people have, no matter how much or how little.

- God can use the insignificant and accomplish the significant.

- Our God is powerful!

Questions

1. Unfortunately, what type of mixed messages do we give our young people?

2. Discuss the "omni" characteristics of God.

- Omniscient

- Omnipresent

- Omnipotent

3. What were the purpose of miracles?

4. How would you explain to people that the age of miracles has ceased?

5. What is the difference between a miracle and a wondrous action?

Chapter 5: Special Friends

As I am sitting at my computer, beginning this chapter … a grown man is on the verge of tears. I am just a few hours away from something I dread.

You may be wondering … Larry, what's wrong? What do you have to do that brings such sadness? So difficult that it brings an old man to tears?

I am just a few hours away from having coffee with two of my very best friends.

You may really be puzzled now … why such dread? Why such sadness? Coffee with friends?

Let me explain.

These guys are two of my best friends. I've known both of them for almost 40 years! These are the friends that are both described by Proverbs 27: 17, "As iron sharpens iron, So a man sharpens the countenance of his friend." Also, Proverbs 18: 24, "A man who has friends must himself be friendly, But there is a friend who sticks closer than a brother."

We have all seen our children grow up together. We've worshipped together. We've shared good times together, and difficult times together. We've been there for each other.

Years ago, the three of us would have "Palm Sundays" together. NO, NO, NO … not the religious Sunday that the world has. No, we each had electronic Palms (that's going back a few years). We would meet before going to worship, have coffee, visit, and share information on our Palms, beaming information to each other.

With one of them, we've been on mission trips on the other side of the globe. He performed the wedding for one of our sons. When my wife was having surgery in a big hospital in a city a couple of hours away, that friend was there. When there would be emergency situations, that friend was there. (When you trust a brother to get you through airports, security, and in a language, you don't even read or understand ... that's trust.)

The other, we've been there for each other. As I said, I've known him for almost 40 years, and our wives have known each other longer than that. It has been a very mutual friendship. When their house burned, we helped. When we were selling a house, we lived with them. One time I was recovering from surgery, and I heard a lawn mower. I looked out the door, and there was this friend, push mowing our lawn. We've helped each other move furniture. We've helped each other take things to the dump. We've taught school together, with our rooms across the hall from each other. (It is amazing how much coffee you can drink, and the conversations that can be had – between classes.) This friend and I have been on two bike rides together, one from Chattanooga to Pigeon Forge, the other from Chattanooga to Argo, Alabama. (How many miles to the gallon did your motorcycles get, you may be wondering? Wait, who said motorcycles – these were bicycles you pedal.)

Emergency hospital stays ... they were there. Needing to stay with my friend after his serious surgery, I was glad to help. I've leaned on this friend for advice, wisdom, and his experiences. He is always, willing to listen.

When they were suffering from Covid, it was a privilege to check on them every day.

We've been to workshops together, shared meals together, shared in good times and serious times.

If you could put all the coffee together, that this friend and I have shared, it would probably fill up a pretty good sized fish pool.

You may be thinking; Larry, these sound like awesome friendships (which they are) so why the sadness, the dread, the verge of tears? Because, one of these friends is getting ready to move about two hours away. This will be the last time the three of us have coffee together, and I don't think I will be able to keep the tears from flowing. These types of friendships are so very special!

In Luke 5, we read of some friendships that must have had the depth and care that my friends and I share. I haven't shared the names of my friends, (some of you who live near me – can probably guess), however from the description you see how special they are. Also, in Luke 5, we don't have the names of the friends shared with us. However, from this obscurity, we find valuable lessons.

Luke 5: 17 – 26, "Now it happened on a certain day, as He was teaching, that there were Pharisees and teachers of the law sitting by, who had come out of every town of Galilee, Judea, and Jerusalem. And the power of the Lord was *present* [a]to heal them. 18 Then behold, men brought on a bed a man who was paralyzed, whom they sought to bring in and lay before Him. 19 And when they could not find how they might bring him in, because of the crowd, they went up on the housetop and let him down with *his* bed through the tiling into the midst before Jesus.

20 When He saw their faith, He said to him, "Man, your sins are forgiven you."

21 And the scribes and the Pharisees began to reason, saying, "Who is this who speaks blasphemies? Who can forgive sins but God alone?"

22 But when Jesus perceived their thoughts, He answered and said to them, "Why are you reasoning in your hearts?23 Which is easier, to say, 'Your sins are forgiven you,' or to say, 'Rise up and

walk'? **24** But that you may know that the Son of Man has power on earth to forgive sins"—He said to the man who was paralyzed, "I say to you, arise, take up your bed, and go to your house."

25 Immediately he rose up before them, took up what he had been lying on, and departed to his own house, glorifying God. **26** And they were all amazed, and they glorified God and were filled with fear, saying, "We have seen strange things today!"

Imagine the place where Jesus was teaching … filled to capacity. The religious folks were there – Pharisee, teachers of the law … coming from every town of Galilee, Judea, and Jerusalem.

However, there were these friends who had a friend in need. He was paralyzed, and they needed to get him to the "Great Physician", Jesus. However, there didn't seem to be a way to get inside.

Somehow, they got him up on the rooftop. Imagine the sounds of tiles being removed, and then a hole in the roof. The friends let their paralyzed friend down, with his bedding, through the roof, right in the midst, before Jesus.

There was no ignoring what had happened. Talk about friendship and determination! Such a valuable lesson, doing all you can to get a friend to Jesus.

When Jesus saw their faith, "He said to him, 'Man your sins are forgiven you.'" Notice, Jesus saw *their* faith, and spoke to the *man*.

Then, notice the religious critics … "And the scribes and the Pharisees began to reason, saying, 'Who is this who speaks blasphemies? Who can forgive sins but God alone?'" (verse 21)

These religious folks accusing the Son of God of blasphemy!

Jesus knew what they were thinking. Jesus answered and said to them, "Why are you reasoning in your hearts? Which is easier, to say, 'Your sins are forgiven you,' or to say, 'Rise up and walk'? But that you may know that the Son of Man has power on earth to forgive sins' – He said to the man who was paralyzed, 'I say to you, arise, take up your bed, and go to your house.'" (verses 22 – 24)

The man who entered by the help of friends, through the rooftop, lying on his bed, exited carrying what he had been lying on, and departed to his own house, glorifying God.

Notice the drastic change in disposition among the crowd from critics to amazement and glorifying God.

"And they were all amazed, and they glorified God and were filled with fear, saying 'We have seen strange things today!'" (verse 26)

- What were the names of these friends? We don't know.

- How long had they known each other? We don't know.

- How had the man become paralyzed? We don't know.

Again, lots of "don't knows", but we sure can learn some valuable lessons from the obscure.

1. The value of true friendships.

2. The importance of getting a friend to Jesus.

3. The power of Jesus manifested.

4. The change in the crowd from critics to glorifiers of God.

"A friend loves at all times, And a brother is born for adversity."
(Proverbs 17: 17)

Questions

1. Describe traits you admire in a friendship.

2. Describe how "friendship evangelism" can be used in bringing a friend to Jesus.

3. What obstacles do we face today in obedience to Jesus?

4. Discuss the power of Jesus being manifested.

5. Discuss the change in attitudes in the crowd.

Chapter 6: The Man with Several Names

This "obscure" character, in *Who? Me ...* has several different names:

- Joseph

- Barsabas

- Justus

He was known by all of these. You may be wondering "Who?".

Let's look at Acts 1: 21 – 26, "Therefore, of these men who have accompanied us all the time that the Lord Jesus went in and out among us, **22** beginning from the baptism of John to that day when He was taken up from us, one of these must become a witness with us of His resurrection."

23 And they proposed two: Joseph called Barsabas, who was surnamed Justus, and Matthias. **24** And they prayed and said, "You, O Lord, who know the hearts of all, show which of these two You have chosen **25** to take part in this ministry and apostleship from which Judas by transgression fell, that he might go to his own place." **26** And they cast their lots, and the lot fell on Matthias. And he was numbered with the eleven apostles."

Judas had sold out and betrayed Jesus. He had thrown the money back, and went out and hanged himself. It had been prophesied that another would take his place as an apostle.

Therefore, two men:

Joseph, Barsabas, Justus

&

Matthias

Both of these men were qualified for the position. The apostles proposed both of them, and prayed, "You, O Lord, who know the hearts of all, show which of these two You have chosen to take part in this ministry and apostleship from which Judas by transgression fell, that he might go to his own place."

Both of these men were proposed. The prayer was that the Lord would show which of these two the Lord had chosen to become an apostle.

The apostles cast their lots, and the lot fell on Mathias. "And he was numbered with the eleven apostles." Mathias was selected by the Lord.

What about Joseph, Barsabas, Justus?

We can learn some valuable lessons by both what is written and what is not written.

1. Joseph, Barsabas, Justus was a qualified man.

2. Joseph, Barsabas, Justus was a faithful follower of Jesus.

3. Joseph, Barsabas, Justus was proposed by the apostles.

However,

4. He was not selected by the Lord for the position of an apostle.

5. We **_do not_** read of him raising objections, complaints, or

ridicule of the apostles, nor rebellion towards God. None of the:

- Why wasn't I selected?

- Why can't both of us serve?

- Well, I guess I'm just not good enough, so forget this.

No complaining, no objections, no rebellion, just submission.

Men, you may have experienced the "second place among two" in the choice selections.

Preachers: maybe you are applying for a position at a congregation, and you are in second place among the choices. Some other man was selected. How are you going to deal with that decision?

Perspective Deacons: maybe you are highly qualified, as far as meeting the qualifications laid out in the Bible. Your name has been submitted to the eldership; however, other men were selected, but you are not in the number of men becoming deacons. How are you going to deal with that decision?

Perspective Elders: maybe you have trained your entire life, desire the office of an elder, meet the qualifications required of an elder, you name has been submitted to the eldership from the congregation to become an elder; however, you are not in the number of men appointed to become one of the shepherds of the congregation. You are disappointed, discouraged, however, how are you going to deal with it?

You may be thinking, Who? Me … acting that way when not being selected, feeling disappointment, feeling rejected, complaining, thinking of "throwing in the towel" and quitting, griping about the eldership, saying derogatory things towards the men selected … Wait, be honest … have those feelings been experienced?

Yet we can definitely learn from the example of the man with several names.

Ladies, what about things you encounter in your lives? What if you have been dating a young man, who you thought was "Mr. Right", then seemingly out of the blue, he informs you that he wants to break up. You feel devastated, disappointed, plans dashed. How do you deal with it?

Ladies, what about if you volunteer to teach a children's class. The selection is made, and you came in "second place" and not selected. You may think, my Bible knowledge exceeds the lady selected. I have experience with children. Why not me?

Ladies, what about if you volunteer to teach a ladies' class. You have studied, know the material that is going to be studied. You are prepared; however, again, "a second-place finish", and another lady is selected for the position. How are you going to deal with it? Complaints, rejection, non-participation, speaking against the teacher selected, causing division, causing discord?

So, ladies … even you can relate and learn from the example from the man with several names.

How easy it is to feel disappointment, rejection, discouragement!

However, a few verses to coincide with the example of the man with several names:

2nd Corinthians 1: 3 – 4, "Blessed *be* the God and Father of our Lord Jesus Christ, the Father of mercies and God of all comfort, [4] who comforts us in all our tribulation, that we may be able to comfort those who are in any [a]trouble, with the comfort with which we ourselves are comforted by God."

Romans 8: 28, "And we know that all things work together for good to those who love God, to those who are the called according to *His* purpose."

Notice Romans 8: 28 says "that all things work together for good to those who love God ..." NOT all things are good. Bad things happen to good people. However, God causes that "all things work together for good to those who love God, to those who are the called according to His purpose."

So, even when things don't seem to go as we want them to; God is in control.

Let's learn to be submissive, obedient, and persevere, in thinking about lessons from the man with several names.

Questions

1. What lessons are apparent to you from the man with several names?

2. How do you overcome rejections and disappointments in life?

3. When you think about being truly submissive to God, what does that mean?

4. How can we use bad things that happen to us to help others?

5. What is the difference between all things working together for good, and all things being good?

Chapter 7: Onesimus

Slavery, the bondage of one man to another is NOT something we like to think about. Age of slavery was a sad time in our history. However, imagine a slave ... and you tell that slave that there are some valuable lessons you can learn from him. He may think, "Who? Me ..." Yes! We can learn lessons from you.

And thus is the case with a slave by the name of Onesimus. We are introduced to him in a very short letter written by the apostle Paul to a man named Philemon. This short epistle to an individual is a one chapter book in the New Testament, only 25 verses.

"Paul, a prisoner of Christ Jesus, and Timothy *our* brother,

To Philemon our beloved *friend* and fellow laborer, **2** to [a]the beloved Apphia, Archippus our fellow soldier, and to the church in your house:

3 Grace to you and peace from God our Father and the Lord Jesus Christ.

4 I thank my God, making mention of you always in my prayers, **5** hearing of your love and faith which you have toward the Lord Jesus and toward all the saints, **6** that the sharing of your faith may become effective by the acknowledgment of every good thing which is in [b]you in Christ Jesus. **7** For we [c]have great [d]joy and [e]consolation in your love, because the [f]hearts of the saints have been refreshed by you, brother.

8 Therefore, though I might be very bold in Christ to command you what is fitting, **9** *yet* for love's sake I rather appeal *to you*—being such a one as Paul, the aged, and now also a prisoner of Jesus Christ— **10** I appeal to you for my son Onesimus, whom I have begotten *while* in my chains, **11** who once was unprofitable to you, but now is profitable to you and to me.

12 I am sending him [g]back. You therefore receive him, that is, my own [h]heart, **13** whom I wished to keep with me, that on your behalf he might minister to me in my chains for the gospel. **14** But without your consent I wanted to do nothing, that your good deed might not be by compulsion, as it were, but voluntary.

15 For perhaps he departed for a while for this *purpose,* that you might receive him forever, **16** no longer as a slave but more than a slave—a beloved brother, especially to me but how much more to you, both in the flesh and in the Lord.

17 If then you count me as a partner, receive him as *you would* me. **18** But if he has wronged you or owes anything, put that on my account. **19** I, Paul, am writing with my own hand. I will repay—not to mention to you that you owe me even your own self besides. **20** Yes, brother, let me have joy from you in the Lord; refresh my heart in the Lord.

21 Having confidence in your obedience, I write to you, knowing that you will do even more than I say. **22** But, meanwhile, also prepare a guest room for me, for I trust that through your prayers I shall be granted to you.

Epaphras, my fellow prisoner in Christ Jesus, greets you, **24** *as do* Mark, Aristarchus, Demas, Luke, my fellow laborers.

25 The grace of our Lord Jesus Christ *be* with your spirit. Amen."

There are three primary lessons we are going to look at from Onesimus:

1. **The difference between the Old Testament and the New Testament.**

2. **The gospel is for all**

3. **The importance of Onesimus**

1. **The difference between the Old Testament and New Testament.**

    Deuteronomy 23: 15, "You shall not give back to his master the slave who has escaped from his master to you."

    Under the Old Testament Law, if a slave had escaped from his master, you were not to give the slave back to his master.

    The Old Law was nailed to the cross.

    Colossians 2: 13 – 14, "And you, being dead in your trespasses and the uncircumcision of your flesh, He has made alive together with Him, having forgiven you all trespasses, **14** having wiped out the [a]handwriting of requirements that was against us, which was contrary to us. And He has taken it out of the way, having nailed it to the cross."

    Paul wrote to Philemon regarding Onesimus, in verses 12 – 14, "I am sending him [7]back. You therefore receive him, that is, my own [8]heart, **13** whom I wished to keep with me, that on your behalf he might minister to me in my chains for the gospel. **14** But without your consent I wanted to do nothing, [h]that your good deed might not be by compulsion, as it were, but voluntary."

    Notice, Paul was sending the slave, Onesimus back to Philemon. If the Old Testament Law was binding at this time, Paul would NOT have been allowed to send Onesimus back to his slave master.

    48

2. The gospel is for all

Paul wrote to Philemon, "I appeal to you for my son Onesimus, whom I have begotten while in my chains," (verse 10)

"For perhaps he departed for a while for this purpose, that you might receive him forever, no longer as a slave but more than a slave – a beloved brother, especially to me but how much more to you, both in the flesh and in the Lord." (verses 15 – 16)

Onesimus, a slave, had obeyed the gospel of Jesus Christ. He was being sent back to Philemon not just a slave, but a brother in Christ.

Acts 2: 37 – 39, Peter's sermon on the Day of Pentecost is recorded, and he said, "Now when they heard *this,* they were cut to the heart, and said to Peter and the rest of the apostles, "Men *and* brethren, what shall we do?"

38 Then Peter said to them, "Repent, and let every one of you be baptized in the name of Jesus Christ for the [a]remission of sins; and you shall receive the gift of the Holy Spirit. **39** For the promise is to you and to your children, and to all who are afar off, as many as the Lord our God will call."

The people had heard the gospel, the death, burial and resurrection of Jesus, and they were guilty of crucifying Jesus. The people interrupted the apostles preaching, as they were cut to the heart and said to Peter and the rest of the apostles, that very important question, "Men and brethren, what shall we do?"

The gospel is for all. Peter told them to "repent and be baptized for the remission of sins; and you shall receive the gift of the Holy Spirit" then said, "For the promise is to you and to your children, and to all who are afar off, as many as the Lord our God will call." (verse 39)

" ... to you and your children" is in reference to Jews. "... to all who afar off, ..." refers to Gentiles.

Romans 1: 16, "For I am not ashamed of the gospel of Christ, for it is the power of God to salvation for everyone who believes, for the Jew first and also for the Greek."

The gospel, God's power of salvation, for everyone who believes, for Jews and Greeks.

This must be an active, obedient belief, not belief alone. James wrote in chapter 2: 19, "You believe that there is one God. You do well. Even the demons believe—and tremble!"

If it was belief only, the demons would be saved. Are the demons saved? Absolutely NOT.

Paul wrote in Galatians 3: 26 – 28, "For you are all sons of God through faith in Christ Jesus. 27 For as many of you as were baptized into Christ have put on Christ. 28 There is neither Jew nor Greek, there is neither slave nor free, there is neither male nor female; for you are all one in Christ Jesus."

(We must be cautious not to put a fence around one verse. A verse is never going to say less than what it says, but there may be more in the context of the passage or found in another passage.)

Some may want to put a fence around verse 26,"For you are

all sons of God through faith in Christ Jesus."

However, can we be saved with Christ Jesus? NO.

How do we put on Christ Jesus? The answer is found in verse 27, "For as many of you as were baptized into Christ have put on Christ."

Then, finding out the gospel is for all, and that all are one in Christ Jesus, verse 28, "There is neither Jew nor Greek, there is neither slave nor free, there is neither male nor female; for you are all one in Christ Jesus."

There are different roles and responsibilities in the Lord's church. There are different functions in the Lord's church. However, the value of the soul is the same in the Lord's church.

Onesimus could return to Philemon, not just as a slave, but a brother in Christ.

3.The importance of Onesimus

As Paul was sending Onesimus back and writing to Philemon, Paul wrote, "I appeal to you for my son Onesimus, whom I have begotten while in my chains, who once was unprofitable to you, but now is profitable to you and to me." (verses 10 – 11)

- Onesimus was once unprofitable to Philemon, but now was profitable to not only Philemon, but also to Paul.

"I am sending him back. You therefore receive him, that is, my own heart, whom I wished to keep with me, that on your behalf he might minister to me in my chains for the gospel." (verses 12 – 13)

- Onesimus would have been beneficial to Paul, "he might minister to me in my chains for the gospel."

- Paul was a Roman prisoner, writing to Philemon.

Therefore, Onesimus was important not only to Paul, but also would be to Philemon.

As we come to the conclusion of this chapter, please think about yourself. Can people learn important things from you?

You may think, "Who? Me …".

1. Can they learn that you are a servant of Jesus Christ?

    Paul wrote in Romans 1: 1, "Paul, a bondservant of Jesus Christ, called to be an apostle, separated to the gospel of God"

    It has previously been discussed in the book, that there are no physically living apostles today, however, there are bondservants of Jesus Christ.

2. Can you share that the gospel of Jesus Christ is for all?

    Are you able to give book, chapter, and verse for answers to that important question of "What must I do to be saved?"?

3. Do you realize that you are important in the kingdom of God?

In First Corinthians 12, Paul used the analogy of the human body, having many members, yet one body for the church; having many members, yet being one body.

You, as a member of the body of Christ, have importance, and a role and function to fill.

Who? ... Me.

You are made in the image of God!

In Genesis 1: 26, "Then God said, "Let Us make man in Our image, according to Our likeness; let them have dominion over the fish of the sea, over the birds of the air, and over the cattle, over [a]all the earth and over every creeping thing that creeps on the earth."

Valuable lessons from Onesimus, that are practical for us:

1. **The difference between the Old Testament and the New Testament.**
   We are living under the New Testament.

2. **The gospel is for all.**
   We need to be ready to share with others the good news of Jesus Christ, being able to answer that important question: "What must I do to be saved?".

3. **You are important.**
   Onesimus was important to Paul, to Philemon, to God. We are important, because we are made in the image of God.

Questions

1. How can a slave have importance?

2. Describe what it means that all are one in Christ Jesus.

3. What can be done in sharing the gospel with all?

4. Give scriptures for God's plan of salvation.

5. How are you important?

Chapter 8: Gaius

How many times have you asked how someone was doing? How many times have you made a call, and said, "Hope you are doing well."? How many texts have you sent, with "Hope you are well."?

How about, wishing someone well in their business efforts? "Hope a financial decision goes well."

However, have you ever wished someone to be doing as well financially or health wise, in correlation to their spirituality? (I don't recall making that type of letter, call, or text.)

Someone must be doing really well spiritually, to wish them well financially, and in health as their soul prospers.

What if that greeting came to you?

Who? Mc ...

Yet, that was exactly the case with the man studied in this chapter; Gaius.

Please read 3ʳᵈ John (one of those one chapter books) verses 1 – 4, "The Elder,

To the beloved Gaius, whom I love in truth:

[2] Beloved, I pray that you may prosper in all things and be in health, just as your soul prospers. [3] For I rejoiced greatly when brethren came and testified of the truth *that is* in you, just as you walk in the truth. [4] I have no greater joy than to hear that my children walk in [a]truth."

Did you notice characteristics of this man?

- "Beloved"

- "Prosper in all things and be in health, just as your soul prospers."

- "For I rejoiced greatly when brethren came and testified of the truth that is in you"

- "Just as you walk in the truth."

- "I have no greater joy than to hear that my children walk in truth."

John, the apostle whom Jesus loved; the apostle who wrote much about love, is calling Gaius "Beloved". What a compliment!

Gaius spirituality was so deep, rich … so much so that John prayed that Gaius "prosper in all things and be in health, just as your soul prospers." What a compliment!

Gaius was a man who had a good report given about him. John rejoiced greatly when "brethren came and testified of the truth that is in you." What a compliment!

Gaius walked in truth. What a compliment!

Gaius brought John encouragement and joy. "I have no greater joy than to hear that my children walk in truth."

This "obscure character" having so many compliments about him, was a man who was bringing encouragement and joy to an apostle.

Not only was Gaius an encouragement to John, the apostle, but also Gaius was an encouragement to brethren as he put his love into action.

Gaius exemplified what John wrote in 1st John 3: 18, "My little children, let us not love in word or in tongue, but in deed and in truth."

Third John verses 5 – 8, "Beloved, you do faithfully whatever you do for the brethren [a]and for strangers, 6 who have borne witness of your love before the church. *If* you send them forward on their journey in a manner worthy of God, you will do well, 7 because they went forth for His name's sake, taking nothing from the Gentiles. 8 We therefore ought to receive[b] such, that we may become fellow workers for the truth."

Gaius put his love into action. He did for others, "brethren and for strangers". He was an example before the church.

Therefore, more valuable lessons from this "obscure character" in the Bible:

- Love in action

- Serving brethren and strangers

- Being an example to the church

We also see the love of Gaius put into action in Romans 16: 23, as Paul writes, "Gaius, my host and the host of the whole church, greets you. Erastus, the treasurer of the city, greets you, and Quartus, a brother."

- The host of Paul

- The host of the whole church.

As we come to the conclusion of this chapter, learning from this "obscure character", that maybe before, not much consideration had been given to him. However, what valuable lessons we can learn from him!

Lessons from Gaius

- He was beloved by John.

- He had a very strong spiritual life.

- He walked in truth.

- He brought joy and encouragement to John.

- He put love into action.

- He served brethren and strangers.

- He was an example to the church.

- He was hospitable.

Questions

1. Would you like to prosper financially, and in health, in correlation to your spiritual life?

2. How can we strengthen our spirituality?

3. What does it mean to "walk in truth"?

4. How can we be examples to the church? (See Matthew 5: 13 – 16, 1st Timothy 4: 12)

5. What lesson from Gaius really stands out to you, or were there other lessons you saw?

Chapter 9: Jason

As my wife and I started having children, we liked Bible names. So, when we were expecting with our firstborn (this was before the days of being able to find out the sex of the baby, and having a reveal party) we had to pick out names for both a boy and a girl. So, looking through a concordance, came across the name Jason, and we both liked that. We did have a baby boy, and he was named Jason.

Three years later, we were expecting our second. We asked our three-year-old, Jason, "If you have a baby brother, what do you want to name him?" He replied, "Nathan.". (He had a little friend in his Bible class with that name.) A Bible name, and we like it. We asked Jason, "What if you have a baby sister, what do you want to name her?" The response, "Nathan.". Good thing he was a boy, and the name Nathan fit.

Back to the name, Jason, the character in the Bible. We are first introduced to him in the book of Acts. Acts 17: 1 – 9, "Now when they had passed through Amphipolis and Apollonia, they came to Thessalonica, where there was a synagogue of the Jews. ² Then Paul, as his custom was, went in to them, and for three Sabbaths reasoned with them from the Scriptures, ³ explaining and demonstrating that the Christ had to suffer and rise again from the dead, and *saying,* "This Jesus whom I preach to you is the Christ." ⁴ And some of them were persuaded; and a great multitude of the devout Greeks, and not a few of the leading women, joined Paul and Silas.

⁵ But the Jews [a]who were not persuaded, [b]becoming envious, took some of the evil men from the marketplace, and gathering a mob, set all the city in an uproar and attacked the house of Jason, and sought to bring them out to the people. ⁶ But when they did not

find them, they dragged Jason and some brethren to the rulers of the city, crying out, "These who have turned the world upside down have come here too. **7** Jason has [c]harbored them, and these are all acting contrary to the decrees of Caesar, saying there is another king—Jesus." **8** And they troubled the crowd and the rulers of the city when they heard these things. **9** So when they had taken security from Jason and the rest, they let them go."

So many times, in the Scriptures, we see that when people are upset with the message, they take it out on the messenger.

Paul reasoned with the Jews from the Scriptures about Jesus. Many were persuaded, but some Jews were not persuaded. They became envious, took some of the evil men from the marketplace and a mob and uproar formed. They "attacked the house of Jason, and sought to bring them out to the people." (verse 5)

They did not find them, so they dragged Jason and some brethren to the rulers of the city. Unknowingly, they gave a compliment, "These who have turned the world upside down have come here too." The Jews made this cry in a mob mentality. Yet, notice the compliment of the spreading of the word of God, and that it had "turned the world upside down".

The mob made accusations about Jason:

- "Jason has harboured them,"

- "and these are all acting contrary to the decrees of Caesar,"

- "saying there is another king – Jesus".

Before letting Jason and the rest to go free, "they had taken security" from them. (verse 9)

In Romans 16, as Paul is concluding the book, gives greetings from various brethren. Among those is Jason. Romans 16: 21, "Timothy, my fellow worker, and Lucius, Jason, and Sosipater, my countrymen, greet you."

Jason was with the apostle, Paul.

Jason:

- A faithful follower of Jesus

- Stood for the truth

- Faced persecution

- Was with the apostle, Paul.

More valuable lessons from an "obscure character" from the Bible. Though not much is said about Jason, what is said shows such conviction, such faithfulness, such strength, such determination, and such concern for souls.

Paul in writing to the young preacher, Timothy, 2nd Timothy 3: 12, "Yes, and all who desire to live godly in Christ Jesus will suffer persecution."

Jason definitely faced persecution!

Questions

1. Those of you having children, what was involved in the selection of your children's names?

2. What can you imagine if you were facing a mob and its mentality?

3. What lesson from Jason gets your attention?

4. Are there other lessons you can think of from the life of Jason?

5. What are some ways we face persecution today?

Chapter 10: Tertius

In WWII, my dad was in the 88th Division, The Blue Devils, as they were known. Dad was in the signal corps. Dad received two purple hearts, and saw some terrible conditions. They had to deliver messages, and if they could not get back to their men, they had to hide and campout, so they could make it back during safer times to travel, and not get shot. Getting those messages to the proper personnel was of utmost importance.

Have you ever been in a situation where an aged person calls you to their bedside, and asks for you to write something for them, as they dictate it? Those words are of utmost importance. You may be thinking ...

"Who? Me ..."

As you are called upon to be the one taking the dictation. The recording of those words, exactly as dictated, is of utmost importance.

My wife, before retiring, worked as a medical transcriptionist for eye surgeons. The surgeons would dictate the notes, messages, or letters to be sent to referring doctors about the treatment. It was extremely important to get the dictation exact, precisely as the surgeon dictated.

- Utmost importance

- Precision

- Exactness

    o All part of the transcription of the dictation.

That brings us to the lesson of Tertius. The obscurity of this character in the Bible may be of such, that you are having to stop and think ... Who is Tertius?.

In the closing of the book of Romans, chapter 16: 22, "I, Tertius, who wrote *this* epistle, greet you in the Lord."

However, we realize that Romans is a Pauline Epistle, a letter written by Paul. Romans 1: 1 – 7, "Paul, a bondservant of Jesus Christ, called *to be* an apostle, separated to the gospel of God [2] which He promised before through His prophets in the Holy Scriptures, [3] concerning His Son Jesus Christ our Lord, who [a]was born of the seed of David according to the flesh, [4] *and* declared *to be* the Son of God with power according to the Spirit of holiness, by the resurrection from the dead. [5] Through Him we have received grace and apostleship for obedience to the faith among all nations for His name, [6] among whom you also are the called of Jesus Christ;

[7] To all who are in Rome, beloved of God, called *to be* saints:

Grace to you and peace from God our Father and the Lord Jesus Christ."

The typical opening of a Pauline Epistle:

- The writer – Paul

- The recipients

- The greeting – grace and peace

So, what did Tertius mean by saying, "I, Tertius, who wrote this epistle, greet you in the Lord."

In other words, he was the scribe for Paul. Paul was doing the dictating, and Tertius was doing the writing. However, it was coming from Paul.

In the Gospel Advocate Commentary on Romans, David Lipscomb wrote, regarding "I Tertius, who write the epistle, salute you in the Lord. – Tertius seems to have been Paul's amanuensis (one who takes dictation). He seldom wrote his epistles with his own hand. He refers to his having written the letter to the Galatians as something unusual: 'See with how large letters I write unto you with mine own hand.' (Gal. 6: 11) At the close of his letters, in order to authenticate them, he usually wrote with his own hand the salutation: 'The salutation of me Paul with mine own hand' (1 Cor. 16: 21); 'The salutation of me Paul with mine own hand, which is the token in every epistle: so I write' (2 Thess. 3: 17)." (Lipscomb)

"Paul sends greetings from eight individuals (Romans 16: 21 – 24)." (Willmington) Among those are "Tertius, the scribe who is writing Romans as Paul dictates it. (Romans 16: 22)" (ibid)

Imagine the trust and confidence that Paul was placing in Tertius to record exactly what Paul was dictating, because "All Scripture *is* given by inspiration of God, and *is* profitable for doctrine, for reproof, for correction, for [a]instruction in righteousness, [17] that the man of God may be complete, thoroughly equipped for every good work." (2nd Timothy 3: 16 – 17)

So little is said about Tertius, yet with that little we understand great lessons:

- The confidence in him by Paul.

- The importance of his work as a scribe.

- The precision of recording what was dictated.

- The exactness of recording what was dictated.

Think about some of the vital lessons in the book of Romans:

- The gospel of Christ – the power of God to salvation (Romans 1: 16)

- "for all have sinned and fall short of the glory of God," (Romans 3: 23)

- "But God demonstrates His own love toward us, in that while we were still sinners, Christ died for us." (Romans 5: 8)

- "Or do you not know that as many of us as were baptized into Christ Jesus were baptized into His death? [4] Therefore we were buried with Him through baptism into death, that just as Christ was raised from the dead by the glory of the Father, even so we also should walk in newness of life." (Romans 6: 3 – 4)

- "For the wages of sin is death, but the gift of God is eternal life in Christ Jesus our Lord." (Romans 6: 23)

- "There is therefore now no condemnation to those who are in Christ Jesus, who do not walk according to the flesh, but according to the Spirit." (Romans 8: 1)

- "Likewise the Spirit also helps in our weaknesses. For we do not know what we should pray for as we ought, but the Spirit Himself makes intercession for us with groanings which cannot be uttered." (Romans 8: 26)

- "What then shall we say to these things? If God is for us, who can be against us?" (Romans 8: 31)

- "Yet in all these things we are more than conquerors through Him who loved us. [38] For I am persuaded that neither death nor life, nor angels nor principalities nor powers, nor things present nor things to come, [39] nor height nor depth, nor any other created thing, shall be able to separate us from the love of God which is in Christ Jesus our Lord." (Romans 8: 37 – 39)

- "I tell the truth in Christ, I am not lying, my conscience also bearing me witness in the Holy Spirit, [2] that I have great sorrow and continual grief in my heart. [3] For I could wish that I myself were accursed from Christ for my brethren, my [a]countrymen according to the flesh," (Romans 9: 1 – 3)

- "Brethren, my heart's desire and prayer to God for [a]Israel is that they may be saved. [2] For I bear them witness that they have a zeal for God, but not according to knowledge. [3] For they being ignorant of God's righteousness, and seeking to establish their own righteousness, have not submitted to the righteousness of God." (Romans 10: 1 – 3)

- "Greet one another with a holy kiss. The churches of Christ greet you." (Romans 16: 16)

The importance of Tertius writing exactly what Paul dictated!

From obscurity, but what vital lessons!

Questions

1. How do you reconcile Paul being the author of the book of Romans and Tertius being the writer of the book of Romans?

2. Discuss the importance of the accuracy of transcription.

3. Discuss Paul's trust in Tertius.

4. What are some of your favorite passages found in the book of Romans?

5. Discuss how valuable lessons can be found from the obscure.

Chapter 11: Lucius

I recently saw a question posted on Facebook asking how many people enjoyed going to a cemetery. There are some people who enjoy that outing and looking at the headstones, dating back to many years ago.

You can gain some information about individuals from what is engraved on those headstones; birthdates, death dates, spouses, maybe other genealogical information. However, one of the things that can easily be taken for granted that is on that headstone ... the dash. That little mark between the date of birth and the date of death. That little dash represents all of the life events of that individual between life and death. Such a small thing, representing so many events, so many activities, so many influences, the things of that person's life ... all represented by that small dash.

This somewhat represents the obscurity of the character in this study; Lucius. Lucius is only mentioned maybe two places in the Bible and when that happens, he is grouped with others. Very little written about him, but yet we can learn some valuable lessons from his life.

Romans 16: 21, "Timothy, my fellow worker, and Lucius, Jason, and Sosipater, my countrymen, greet you."

From this brief passage we can learn:

- Lucius was with the apostle Paul.

- Lucius cared about fellow brothers and sisters in Christ, as he was sending a greeting to the beloved saints in Rome.

- Lucius had some powerful, positive influences surrounding him. Timothy, Paul's son in the faith; Jason, who we have already studied in this book; Sosipater … Paul's countrymen.

Paul wrote in 1st Corinthians 15: 33, "Do not be deceived: Evil company corrupts good habits."

Lucius was NOT surrounding himself with evil company!

Rather, the passage in Proverbs 27: 17, seems much more appropriate for Lucius and his associations, "As iron sharpens iron, So a man sharpens the countenance of his friend."

Another passage where we read about Lucius is found in Acts 13: 1 – 3, "Now in the church that was at Antioch there were certain prophets and teachers: Barnabas, Simeon who was called Niger, Lucius of Cyrene, Manaen who had been brought up with Herod the tetrarch, and Saul. ² As they ministered to the Lord and fasted, the Holy Spirit said, "Now separate to Me Barnabas and Saul for the work to which I have called them." ³ Then, having fasted and prayed, and laid hands on them, they sent *them* away."

In the *Gospel Advocate Commentary on Romans* regarding Lucius, "**and Lucius** – Lucius of Cyrene in mentioned (Acts 13: 1) as one of the prophets and teachers at Antioch who were called upon to separate Paul and Barnabas for the work among the Gentiles. This is probably the same." (Lipscomb)

As the Lord was convincing Ananias to go to Saul, the Lord told Ananias regarding Saul, "… Go, For he is a chosen vessel of Mine to

bear My name before Gentiles, kings, and the children of Israel."
(Acts 9: 15)

Imagine having a part in fulfilling the Lord's plans, in setting apart
Barnabas and Saul for the work among the Genitles.

From Acts 13, we discover things about Lucius: (including Barnabas,
Simeon who was called Niger, Manaen, and Saul).

- Prophet
  - From the Greek, meaning an inspired speaker.
    (Meyer)

- Teacher

- Ministered to the Lord

- Fasted and prayed

- " ... the Holy Spirit said, 'Now separate to Me Barnabas and
  Saul for the work to which I have called them.'"

What a powerful group of men!

Think of the submission of these men, the obedience of these men,
the faithfulness of these men. (More valuable lessons!)

What if you had been called upon before reading this chapter, write
out some things about Lucius. You may have thought, **Who? Me ...**

Yet from this obscure character, little written about him, yet we can
learn some very valuable lessons!

Questions

1. What are you learning from looking at obscure characters, including Lucius, and finding some valuable lessons?

2. Discuss some traits and characteristics that stand out to you about Lucius.

3. Discuss the blessing and the power of prayer, because of our powerful, living GOD.

4. Discuss the dangers of associating with evil companions.

5. Discuss the blessings of being around fellow Christians.

Chapter 12: Jael

The Israelites had a life cycle:

- Sin

- Suffering

- Sorrow

- Salvation

- Sin

- Suffering

- Sorrow

- Salvation

Again, again, and again.

Judges 4: 1, "When Ehud was dead, the children of Israel again did evil in the sight of the Lord."   (Sin)

Judges 4: 2, "So the Lord sold them into the hand of Jabin king of Canaan, who reigned in Hazor. The commander of his army was Sisera, who dwelt in Harosheth Hagoyim.   (Suffering)

Judges 4: 3, "And the children of Israel cried out to the LORD; for Jabin had nine hundred chariots of iron, and for twenty years he had harshly oppressed the children of Israel."   (Sorrow)

Judges 4: 4, "Now Deborah, a prophetess, the wife of Lapidoth, was judging Israel at that time." (Beginning of the salvation of the Israelites from bondage.)

There are some characters to remember in this account:

- Jabin – king of Canaan

- Sisera – commander of the army of Jabin

- Deborah – prophetess, judge, wife of Lapidoth

- Lapidoth – husband of Deborah

- Barak – "leader" of the troops of Israel

- Heber – father-in-law (brother-in-law; depending on the translators) of Moses.

- Jael – wife of Heber

The Israelites were harshly oppressed by Jabin, king of Canaan. Sisera was the commander of his strong, nine hundred chariots of iron, people that were with him, strong.

Deborah told Barak, the "leader" of the troops of Israel, "Has not the Lord God of Israel commanded, 'Go and deploy troops at Mount Tabor; take with you ten thousand men of the sons of Naphtali and of the sons of Zebulun; and against you I will deploy Sisera, the commander of Jabin's army, with his chariots and his multitude at the River Kishon; and I will deliver him into your hand?" (Judges 4: 6 – 7)

God had told Barak, to "Go and deploy troops …" and God was going to give the victory, " … I will deliver him into your hand". However, the "leader" was hesitant, and had to be encouraged by the wife of Lapidoth, Deborah.

Watch this "leader" Barak's response … "If you will go with me, then I will go; but if you will not go with me, I will not go!" (verse 8)

Wait … Barak … hasn't God commanded you to go? Hasn't God promised you the victory? Hasn't God said he would give the victory? Hasn't God said, "I will deliver him into your hand"? Why are you waiting???

So, this "leader" said to Deborah, "If you will go with me, then I will go; but if you will not go with me, I will not go!" (Now readers, you see why "leader" is in quotations marks.)

"So she said, 'I will surely go with you; nevertheless there will be no glory for you in the journey you are taking, for the Lord will sell Sisera into the hand of a woman.' Then Deborah arose and went with Barak to Kedesh. And Barak called Zebulun and Naphtali to Kedesh; he went up with ten thougsand me under his command, and Deborah went up with him." (verses 9 – 10)

"Now Heber the Kenite, of the children of Hobab the father-in-law of Moses, had separated himself from the Kenites and pitched his tent near the terebinth tree at Zaanaim, which is beside Kedesh." (Verse 11).

Sisera gathered together his strong army. It took Deborah to tell the "leader", "Up! For this is the day in which the Lord has delivered Sisera into your hand. Has not the Lord gone out before you? ' So Barak went down from Mount Tabor with ten thousand men following him." (Verses 13 – 14)

"And the Lord routed Sisera and all *his* chariots and all *his* army with the edge of the sword before Barak; and Sisera alighted from *his* chariot and fled away on foot. **16** But Barak pursued the chariots and the army as far as Harosheth Hagoyim, and all the army of Sisera fell by the edge of the sword; not a man was left." (verses 15 – 16)

Sisera was on the run! He ran to the tent of Jael, the wife of Heber. The account in verses 18 – 20, "And Jael went out to meet Sisera, and said to him, "Turn aside, my lord, turn aside to me; do not fear." And when he had turned aside with her into the tent, she covered him with a [e]blanket.

19 Then he said to her, "Please give me a little water to drink, for I am thirsty." So she opened a jug of milk, gave him a drink, and covered him. **20** And he said to her, "Stand at the door of the tent, and if any man comes and inquires of you, and says, 'Is there any man here?' you shall say, 'No.' "

Jael:

Got Sisera into her tent.

Got him comfortable, covered him with a blanket.

Sisera asked for water, she gave him milk.

Sisera told her to stand by the door of the tent, and if any man asked about a man inside, Sisera wanted her to lie and say 'no'.

Sisera fell asleep.

Verse 21, "Then Jael, Heber's wife, took a tent peg and took a hammer in her hand, and went softly to him and drove the peg into his temple, and it went down into the ground; for he was fast asleep and weary. So he died."

Jael, this obliging, hospitable, wife of Heber, drove a tent peg through the temple of Sisera, killing him.

Remember, Barak was pursuing Sisera. Barak arrived at the tent of Jael. "Jael came out to meet him, and said to him, 'Come, I will show you the man whom you seek.' And when he went into her tent, there lay Sisera, dead with the peg in his temple." (verse 22)

"So on that day God subdued Jabin king of Canaan in the presence of the children of Israel." (verse 23)

Remember, Deborah had told Barak there would be no glory for him, "for the Lord will sell Sisera into the hand of a woman." (verse 9)

Then, Deborah and Barak sang on that day. The song gave praise to the Lord. Deborah, and the "leader of the troops of Israel", Barak sang:

"24 "Most blessed among women is Jael,
The wife of Heber the Kenite;
Blessed is she among women in tents.
25 He asked for water, she gave milk;
She brought out cream in a lordly bowl.
26 She stretched her hand to the tent peg,
Her right hand to the workmen's hammer;
She pounded Sisera, she pierced his head,
She split and struck through his temple.
27 At her feet he sank, he fell, he lay still;
At her feet he sank, he fell;
Where he sank, there he fell dead." (Judge 5: 24 – 27)

God used this obscure, obliging, hospitable, wife of Heber, in the privacy of her tent, to drive a tent peg through the temple of Sisera, killing the commander of the might army of Jabin, king of Canaan.

Questions

1. Who do you think showed more bravery, Deborah or Barak?

2. Give examples of God using the insignificant in God giving victory of what appears from human perspectives, as insurmountable odds.

3. What encouragement did it take for Barak to go into action?

4. How can we encourage one another to go into action for God?

5. Discuss how God used an obliging, hospitable, wife to kill Sisera, the commander of the mighty army of Jabin the king of Canaan.

Chapter 13: Jochebed

Have you felt like you have lost your own identity? *Who? Me ...*

Parents: Have you gone to a school activity, open house, ball game or whatever, and you are introduced as the parents of your child? Your child is known ... you are the parents of that child, however it's like you have lost your own identity by not being called by your own name.

Husbands: Have you ever gone to your wife's work place? You are introduced as your wife's husband ... not necessarily by your own name ... feeling like just maybe ... you've lost a little of your own identity.

Wives: Have you ever gone somewhere your husband is known, but not you? Perhaps you've gone to one of his office events. Perhaps you are the wife of a preacher, and introduced as his wife. Maybe you've gone to that little league game, or some other ball game, and introduced as that boy or girl's mom. What about your own identity?

Children: Oh ... you can relate to this one! You go to that family reunion. You are introduced as your mom and dad's child, and that dear aunt squeezes you on the cheek, telling you how she's known you since you were just a very little baby. What about your own identity?

However, this is NOT all bad, especially, if your child is well known for good behavior, a husband achieves because of the support of his wife, the wife is loved and honored by a godly husband, children are loved, nurtured and brought up properly!

Such is the case in the "hall of fame of heroes of faith" in Hebrews chapter 11. There are some individuals that are mentioned, but not by name. You may be thinking ... oh, near the end of the chapter verses 35 – 40,

"Women received their dead raised to life again. And others were tortured, not accepting deliverance, that they might obtain a better resurrection.
36 Still others had trial of mockings and scourgings, yes, and of chains and imprisonment.
37 They were stoned, they were sawn in two, were tempted, were slain with the sword. They wandered about in sheepskins and goatskins, being destitute, afflicted, tormented--
38 of whom the world was not worthy. They wandered in deserts and mountains, in dens and caves of the earth.
39 And all these, having obtained a good testimony through faith, did not receive the promise,
40 God having provided something better for us, that they should not be made perfect apart from us."

Granted, there are definitely individuals mentioned, but not by name. However, there is another reference, back a few verses, and from other passages, we can find exactly who they are.

Hebrews 11: 23, "By faith Moses, when he was born, was hidden three months by his parents, because they saw *he was* a beautiful child; and they were not afraid of the king's command."

Moses is mentioned!

Moses is mentioned. However, look at the verse carefully ... "his parents".

We find the name of Moses' parents in Exodus 6: 20, "Now Amram took for himself Jochebed, his father's sister, as wife; and she bore him Aaron and Moses. And the years of the life of Amram *were* one hundred and thirty-seven."

Amram and Jochebed were the parents of Moses. In this chapter, we want to spend some time looking at the life of Jochebed.

Exodus 2: 1 – 10, "And a man of the house of Levi went and took *as wife* a daughter of Levi. ²So the woman conceived and bore a son. And when she saw that he *was* a beautiful *child,* she hid him three months. ³But when she could no longer hide him, she took an ark of bulrushes for him, daubed it with asphalt and pitch, put the child in it, and laid *it* in the reeds by the river's bank. ⁴And his sister stood afar off, to know what would be done to him.

⁵Then the daughter of Pharaoh came down to bathe at the river. And her maidens walked along the riverside; and when she saw the ark among the reeds, she sent her maid to get it. ⁶And when she opened *it,* she saw the child, and behold, the baby wept. So she had compassion on him, and said, "This is one of the Hebrews' children."

⁷Then his sister said to Pharaoh's daughter, "Shall I go and call a nurse for you from the Hebrew women, that she may nurse the child for you?"

⁸And Pharaoh's daughter said to her, "Go." So the maiden went and called the child's mother. ⁹Then Pharaoh's daughter said to her, "Take this child away and nurse him for me, and I will give *you* your wages." So the woman took the child and nursed him. ¹⁰And the child grew, and she brought him to Pharaoh's daughter, and he became her son. So she called his name [a]Moses, saying, "Because I drew him out of the water."

Imagine this mom of two children, Aaron and Miriam. Now she is expecting another baby. The command has gone out from Pharaoh regarding the Israelite slaves, "Every son who is born you shall cast into the river, and every daughter you shall save alive." (Exodus 1: 22)

This was definitely before imaging to determine the sex of a baby. (That wasn't even around in 1980 or 1983, when our babies were born. You waited nine months to find out if you had a son or daughter.)

So, the command has gone from Pharaoh, so now what??? If it is a boy, he is supposed to be killed. If it is a daughter, she is allowed to live.

Jochebed had the baby, a baby boy, and "she saw that he was a beautiful child, she hid him three months." (Exodus 2: 2)

How did she hide him for three months? How was she able to give this baby boy all that he needed to eat or drink? How was she able to muffle the crying?

We aren't given all the details.

However, the time came when she could no longer hide him. She prepared the "ark of bulrushes" and "laid it in the reeds by the river's bank." (Verse 3)

The little ark was seen by Pharaoh's daughter. She sent her maid to get the ark. When Pharaoh's daughter opened the ark, the baby boy cried. She had compassion on the baby, and realized he was one of the Hebrews' children.

Notice God's providence in action:

- Why was it Pharaoh's daughter who came to bathe?

- Why was it that she saw the ark?

- Why did the baby boy cry when the ark was opened?

- Why did she have compassion, even when her father had commanded that all the baby boys were to be killed?

84

- The baby boy's mother was able to nurse her own child with permission from Pharaoh's daughter.

"And the child grew, and she brought him to Pharaoh's daughter, and he became her son. So she called his name Moses, saying 'Because I drew him out of the water.'" (Verse 10)

Don't you know that had to be a difficult day for Jochebed to deliver her son to Pharaoh's daughter, to become her son, and she was the one to name him?

Yet, all that transpired, all the years, all the actions, all the events, and Moses becoming the "man of God" (Deuteronomy 33: 1), "the servant of the Lord" (from many passages in the Bible), the leader of God's people ... leading them out of Egyptian bondage and to the promised land, though he was not allowed to enter because of his disobedience to God, not giving God the glory at the rock, and striking it instead of speaking to it. (There are consequences for disobedience, no matter who commits the sin.)

Stop and think ... how could this all have happened, God's plan carried out, had it not been from an obscure, woman of faith, and obedience to God, Jochebed?

Questions

1. With the loss of our own personal identity, how can God be glorified?

2. What are some traits of Jochebed are that are valuable to you?

3. What traits did Jochebed demonstrate by hiding her baby boy, nursing her baby boy, and giving her baby boy to Pharaoh's daughter?

4. What is the reward of Jochebed's faith?

5. What are some lessons we can learn from Jochebed to strengthen our own faith?

Chapter 14: Summary

It is so easy in our society, our culture, our routines … to sell ourselves short. Whether it is because of television, movies, mass media, peer pressure … we often have the wrong standard for measurement. We forget that we are made in the image of God.

It is so easy to see our shortcomings, our frailties, our inadequacies, and think

Who? Me …

In Matthew 25, we read of the parable of the talents. One servant was given five, another two, and another one talent. The "one talent man" was NOT condemned because he only had one talent. He was condemned because he did not use what he had been given. He was not judged according to the "five talent man", nor the "two talent man". He was not judged by what he did not have, but how he had used what he did have.

A reminder about the cover of the book, and the photograph of the lighthouse – when you think …

Who? Me …

Matthew 5: 13 – 16, "You are the salt of the earth; but if the salt loses its flavor, how shall it be seasoned? It is then good for nothing but to be thrown out and trampled underfoot by men.

[14] "You are the light of the world. A city that is set on a hill cannot be hidden. [15] Nor do they light a lamp and put it under a basket, but on a lampstand, and it gives light to all *who are* in the house. [16] Let your light so shine before men, that they may see your good works and glorify your Father in heaven."

Christians, we are the salt of the earth, a city on a hill that cannot be hidden, the light of the world. You may be like a lighthouse, showing the way to Jesus to others.

There are times we feel we are not capable for the task at hand. We become fearful, doubtful, and lose focus. We feel so inadequate, so obscure, and think ...

Who? Me ...

However, after reading this book, using it as a tool in studying your Bible, and learning lessons from characters we have studied ...

- Grandpa
- A Servant Girl
- Mariners
- A Lad
- Special Friends
- The Man with Several Names
- Onesimus
- Gaius
- Jason
- Tertius
- Lucius
- Jael
- Jochebed

Maybe, just maybe, it will be an encouragement in overcoming the …

Who? Me …

syndrome and complex.

26 Then God said, "Let Us make man in Our image, according to Our likeness; let them have dominion over the fish of the sea, over the birds of the air, and over the cattle, over [a]all the earth and over every creeping thing that creeps on the earth." **27** So God created man in His *own* image; in the image of God He created him; male and female He created them." (Genesis 1: 26 – 27)

Questions

1. What can we do to overcome things in our society that cause us to lose focus?

2. What was a favourite chapter in the book, and why?

3. How can we utilize the "talents" God has given us, according to His will?

4. Describe some ways God has used the obscure to His glory.

5. Reflect and discuss what it means to be made in the "image of God".

Notes

References

Biblia.com, NKJV, internet.

Biblestudytools.com, internet.

Concordance, *The Holy Bible,* New King James Version, Copyright 1982 by Thomas Nelson, Inc.

Gillen, A., *Answeringensis.org, "Biblical Leprousy: Shedding Light on the Disease that Shuns,* June 10, 2007, October 25, 2009.

Lipscomb, D.; *A Commentary on the New Testament Epistles, Romans;* Gospel Advocate Company, Nashville, Tenn., 1989.

Meyer, R.; *e-Sword LT*

Record of Deaths, *The Holy Bible,* New King James Version, Copyright 1982 by Thomas Nelson, Inc.

Safari Search Engine, Internet.

Search.yahoo.com powered by *Oxford Dictionaries.*

StudyLight.org; *Coffman Commentaries on the Bible,* 2nd Kings 5.

The Holy Bible, New King James Version, Copyright 1982 by Thomas Nelson, Inc.

Willmington, H.; *The Outline Bible;* Tyndale House Publishers, Inc., Wheaton, IL, 1999.

Women of the Old Testament, "Jochebed".

www.biblegateway.com, New King James Version.

www.geni.com

Made in the USA
Columbia, SC
04 July 2023